POTTY TRAINING FOR BOYS IN 3 DAYS

STEP-BY-STEP GUIDE TO GET YOUR TODDLER
DIAPER FREE. NO-STRESS TOILET TRAINING

SAMANTHA KIMELL

CONTENTS

INTRODUCTION

Having children is a wonderful experience for parents around the world. Children bring some wonderful memories, but what stands out among the more challenging memories is changing messy diapers. This is a chore that no parent appreciates, and figuring out how to teach your child to use the potty can be very difficult, particularly if having a system in place has not been at the top of your priority list.

In this book, we will look at a few of the most efficient methods for potty training your boy to ensure that he comprehends everything and will use the potty. Teaching children how to go to the potty and knowing when to begin potty training is something that most parents feel unsure of. There are numerous potty-training strategies, and it is important to choose the right one for your child. Whether he learns or not will depend on his desire and willingness to cooperate.

Don't begin potty training too quickly. Studies show that when parents begin potty training too early, their children take more time to master the skill. So you will have potty-training success when your child is ready to start the training.

The first thing you will need to do is to use the information in this book to check whether your child is ready to be potty trained. When he is ready, concentrate on the planning. Ensure your child's routine is simple. If he has begun daycare recently or has a younger brother or sister, he might be less responsive to change. Wait until he feels more open to transition in order for potty training to be a success.

One way to pinpoint when your toddler is ready to be potty trained is to look for signs of readiness. These signs range from hunching down and grunting, to remaining dry for three hours or more. When you know and recognize these common indications of potty training readiness, you can choose when to prepare your child to use the potty. Don't potty train your child before he is ready!

Please note this: No child can be toilet trained until he is ready. Your child holds all the power in this situation. He can be gently guided, but not forced to use the toilet. Toilet training is about patience, calmness, and guiding your child to figure things out for himself.

CHAPTER 1. BACKGROUND

Some parents ask, "Why bother potty training? Doesn't it just fall into place naturally?" Or they think that if a child is presented with the routine of potty training early, he will learn to go to the toilet by himself. However, that isn't the case.

Many individuals feel that older children (four plus years) potty train quicker than children who are prepared at a younger age (one-three years). Some presumptions that sometimes come from the medical profession, contemporary childcare, or the community are:

✓ Children can't accomplish successful toilet training until the "myelination of the sphincters" takes place and efforts to toilet train them before this time will be purposeless.

✓ All toddlers wind up getting toilet trained eventually

anyway—did you ever observe an adult who isn't toilet trained?

✓ Children can prepare themselves when they are four years old.

✓ No child in secondary school is in diapers…

It's true there are some toddlers who "prepare themselves." These are children who grow up in a home where parents make the potty or toilet facilities accessible to their kids from birth, while not deliberately calling it "training."

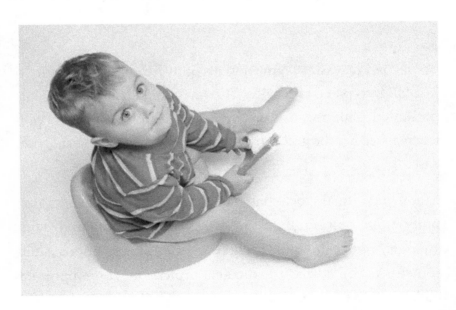

In any case, if we are talking about the development of a one-and-a-half to a three-year-old child who is not yet potty-prepared, he isn't ready to train himself. Unfortunately, some parents are constrained by work or social situations and can't play a dynamic part in helping their child get potty trained, even after they figure out what their child needs.

Potty training is an essential exercise to train a child's body to enjoy the benefits of what is sometimes called man's most important invention ever—indoor plumbing/sanitation. Figuring out how to take oneself to the bathroom is one of the crucial requirements for lifelong health.

The physical capabilities of your child to be potty trained fall into place easily; however, like all areas where the body meets hardware, essential training is required. We get excited about our infant's first word, his first tooth and his first steps (tears of joy!), but we flinch at the possibility of cleaning up the messes needed to enable our child to learn self-toileting. Diapers, pull-ups, cushioned pants, and the like keep the pee and poop out of everyone's sight for a very long time.

But if we give potty training a second look, we will discover that it's a means to a fundamental end, as well as an opportunity to bond with our child. Its advantages touch areas of life well beyond the potty.

Potty Training Around the World

While we battle to balance work and parenting, we don't want to discuss potty training our kids; the subject is deemed to be gross or unsavory. But that hasn't been the case with our neighbors in other parts of the world, and it still isn't today.

Moms outside the western world may be astounded at all the fuss around potty training. They appear to know intuitively when to potty train because they hold their children close to their bodies more often than not.

When you're carrying your child on your side, these signals are difficult to miss. If they are fifteen feet away on a mat, it's a lot easier to miss them. African and Asian ladies carry their children throughout the day, so they naturally know when the time has come to hold their newborn children out away from them so they can relieve themselves.

In a large part of Europe, parents say that infants give signals that let you know when they have to go, so they don't use diapers throughout the day. In Germany, the potty is made available; however, toddlers are permitted to go at their own pace. In France, no child begins school in diapers, and they aren't permitted in playgroups in diapers at one-three years old.

In China and India, parents begin the potty-training process early. When babies are one year old, their parents or caregivers routinely hold them over the potty after the main meal and make a suggestive "shhh-shee" sound for peeing, or "uh, uh" to help an infant poop. This takes some time, but once the children catch on, they do both without fail. In China, little kids regularly wear pants with a split in the back through which they can relieve themselves.

In societies where parents keep their very young toddlers near them, the parents learn to read their child's signals.

The child certainly adapts, but the main person who is prepared is the parent. Parents who attempt "sans diaper" techniques from birth are committed, and it is something all parents could do if they wanted.

In Japan, bowel movements are firmly associated with health and well-being, so discussion of potty training is common. They even have cartoons and kids' books to instruct both parents and children about the advantages of using the potty.

A typical feature among every one of these mothers is that they are accustomed to starting potty training earlier rather than later. This is important because they use terrycloth or birdseye cotton diapers more than the super-absorbent disposables. The child shows discomfort in dirty or wet diapers faster and this in itself serves as a signal to start potty training.

The History of Potty Training

Diaper material has long been a controlling factor in the area of potty-training. Getting kids out of diapers quickly was necessary when diapers were made from cloth or cotton wool. For a pioneer mother with unlimited heaps of clothing and wet diapers to dry (often without washing them), there was no discussion about when to begin potty training. It was best to teach toddlers to go in the chamber pot as early as possible. This occasionally prompted outrageous measures utilizing bowel purges and suppositories.

Washing machines helped ease mothers' burdens in the 1950's. However, mothers still were using cloth diapers, so they were still attentive to their child's schedules and signals and would put them on the potty when the child was expected to go. The child would then make the association between his signals and being placed on the potty. It was normal for children to be potty trained by 18 months.

In the 1980s, disposable diapers became significantly more affordable. Parents could choose either cloth diapers or disposables. Soon, parents were no longer as overly energetic to potty train their toddlers at an early age.

This was around the time that pediatrician Dr. T. Brazelton Berry and the American Academy of Pediatrics upheld a potty-training approach, which was a reaction to the fairly unforgiving schedules utilized in the previous century. Rather than rushing, parents were urged to wait until the child could convey his needs. Gradually, the focus moved from the parents' needs to the child's needs.

Today, the pendulum has swung completely away from early potty training. Disposable diapers are not just an option but are the standard. With more moms working outside the home, and diapers more reasonably priced, we aren't propelled to potty train our kids simply to lessen our workload. Potty training is not a need. Today we see nothing wrong with children wearing diapers well into the toddler years.

The idea of efficiently potty training children under one

year old has been completely given up in western countries like Australia, the U.S., the U.K., and many countries in Europe. The more common view now is that it is okay to postpone potty training until after three years of age.

In any case, late potty training brings about a slower development of a child's other learning abilities. The consistent counsel of present-day childcare consultants to "wait until the toddler is prepared" can be careless because most parents aren't properly equipped to recognize when their child is prepared.

Many parents depend on rewards rather than on instructing their kids to be free in using the potty. This may work for some, but regularly produces stressed, over-the-top haggling between parent and child, particularly with children who have discovered how to express their rebellion in words, or who refuse to go along when rewards are no longer given. Also, haggling is absolutely ineffective.

Others approach potty training as a mystery, with no structure and with little regard for the toddler's signals. The drawback is that, though this resembles training, it will take longer as both parent and child get disappointed when there doesn't appear to be any lasting progress with this approach.

Finally, there are individuals who avoid the learning of pottying skills and fall back on commercial products to address potty needs. Who wouldn't think that it's less demanding to put a disposable diaper on a tyke than to apply the effort to train him?

On the off chance that somebody has missed the point of who is pushing this change in potty training, it's the diaper manufacturers. They have profited by dragging out diaper use in older children, even making additional larger sized diapers for children up to four and five years of age. As a result, the normal potty-training age in America has now moved to 30 months (but can go as high as 60 months)!

There is also less impetus toward potty training for parents as well as for children since disposables keep dampness far from the skin. Infants and little children don't recognize what it feels like to be wet.

Research indicates that around 90 percent of American kids wear disposables, and only around 10 percent are potty trained by a year and a half, though it was not that long ago that 95 percent of children were potty trained by a year and a half, even without the unforgiving potty-training techniques of the mid-1900s.

At What Age Should Children Today Be Potty Trained?

Around the world, half of all children are potty trained by the time they are one year old; some even by six months. The vast majority of the world's kids are potty trained by age two. In the U.S., most boys are not potty trained until 35 to 39 months of age (around three years old).

This troubling pattern has not gone unnoticed. Child healthcare services have distributed broad reports and recommendations about how to turn this around. However, at the same time that first world nations address the issue of later potty training, the pattern of giving up the custom of early potty training is in full swing among the white-collar class of China and other more recently-developing nations.

In Hong Kong, it is still common to try to avoid the long-term use of diapers. In China, despite all of its advances, people still wish to avoid depending on diapers since they are still very costly there. But now that more Chinese individuals are getting wealthier, there is a higher demand for diapers.

Nowadays, instead of people thinking that it's bizarre that a school-age boy isn't yet potty-trained, they frown on parents who train their kid sooner than two years of age. One mother who started potty training her child before he was two explained that people were extremely critical of her for doing that, saying it was "too soon."

Control of bodily elimination is a vital part of human development. It is the earliest self-control learned by small children. Today, toddlers learn how to utilize complex electronic gadgets at ages when they previously accomplished continence.

Potty Training for Today's Needs

The essential element for a successful potty-training technique is lots of love. Love makes the difference between harsh methods and healthy methods. The best strategies are those that encourage, not enforce, potty training, but at the same time are sufficiently firm to make a stamp on a kid's muscle memory.

We will take some time to rediscover what mothers in our country and around the globe have known from the beginning. We'll combine the best from different sources to see how we can best teach our children.

Motivations for Early Potty Training

In Japan, parents are motivated to potty train their kids early in order to diminish the burden on others; such as friends, instructors, or childcare providers. The more children that come to class in diapers, the more the instruction time suffers.

Preschool educators who have untrained three-year-olds in class lose time changing diapers when they could be teaching. This is difficult, particularly for educators who come from countries where toddlers can't begin nursery or preschool unless they are potty trained. One instructor expressed, "I believe it's ridiculous not to attempt to get toddlers out of diapers by three years of age."

At the same time, children who have had fundamental potty training at home can fill in as supportive copycat models for schoolmates who may be uncertain how to help themselves. Two, three, and four-year-olds learn quickly when they see others using the toilet. Their consistent pattern makes a difference.

Clean and Sterile

Commonsense parents who begin potty training when their kids are between one and three years of age find it cleaner, less expensive, and well-timed to the autonomy and independent development of the child. They don't spend a lot of time thinking about it, they just start potty-training when they see that their children are prepared. They don't start out fearing it will be a difficult undertaking, rather they just lead the way in starting and supporting their child.

They never again need to keep cleaning up after their toddlers. These parents feel that western society has retrogressed by keeping kids in diapers longer. They believe a toddler needs consistent close encouragement and training so sterile potty training can happen without the use of diapers. There's no question that it's cleaner and more agreeable for a toddler to be potty trained early.

Good for the Environment

There's also no doubt about what is better for nature—getting your kid out of diapers early eliminates a ton of waste. The ecological contamination from cloth diapers is less than that of disposables. A normal child is changed six to eight times each day. That is around 3,000 disposable diapers for each child per year!

Disposable diapers create a huge volume of waste as they are sometimes tossed in residential recycling receptacles;

their waste contaminates the other post-consumer paper and renders it unfit to reuse.

Disposable diapers are additionally a litter issue on shore-lines, and in regions where there are few or no public trash bins.

Less Expensive, Less Strain on the Budget

Parents who can manage the cost of disposables more often than not potty train later, while budget-conscious parents tend to train earlier. Regardless of economic need, parents who prepare early get the special reward of a completely potty trained child sooner than the individuals who simply rely on diapers.

More Parental Attention to the Child

Potty training is a great way for parents to give their children a greater amount of attention and support as they work toward the end goal.

While full-time homemakers are in the greatest position to potty train their children, working moms have an extra motivation compared to non-working moms to give the required attention and support. Working moms who decide to potty train early appreciate the lower maintenance and other advantages that this choice brings. Those who don't train early lose those advantages.

This training is also an opportunity to bond with your child.

What's more, we can see its positive impact on family relationships.

Supports a Toddler's Self-sufficiency and Autonomy

Although many parents are worried about the intellectual development of their children and less worried about their toddlers being in diapers, many moms have seen the link between the self-control learned in potty training and the general advancement of their child.

Lessens Future Health Problems

There are numerous other benefits brought about by potty training. These include decreasing the rate of lower urinary tract disease and a ruptured bladder, incessant constipation, and colon issues.

What happens to those who don't potty-train early?

✓ Unnecessary embarrassment.

✓ No clear idea of when to stop using diapers.

✓ Health problems.

✓ Struggle to potty train at a later age.

A Healthy Method

What we are shooting for is a healthy potty-training method which includes every one of the conditions required for correct training. Training for parents, reacting to the kid's needs, preparing the body and brain, and perceiving regular signs are all part of this. Now it's a matter of bringing the issues to light so that parents can see that it is best to begin potty training between one—three years of age.

This can be a smooth and seamless process, unlike training during the "terrible twos," when children declare their independence and may use potty training as an act of insubordination.

The Effectiveness of the Three-Day Method

Potty training in a brief timeframe works well for many parents, though it isn't currently the normal pattern. The Three-Day Method in this book has helped countless children make that all-important leap forward from wearing diapers. It has also helped many parents become more acquainted with their children outside of the daily routine and workload.

Using this or other training techniques doesn't necessarily mean that your child will be completely potty trained in three days. Rather, in three days, your child will be using the potty as opposed to diapers.

Nevertheless, there may be accidents and you'll have to establish a reliable potty routine—helping your child utilize the potty freely, showing him how to pull his pants down, flush the potty, and wash his hands—until one day he's doing it with no accidents!

Having a child learn to use the potty in three days may sound too good to be true. However, it truly takes toddlers who are around two years old only three days to get the basics of potty-training. A few kids get it quicker than that, particularly those whose parents are consistent and organized before the actual "Three Days."

Potty training is more complicated than just taking off the diaper and giving your toddler some instructions, but in spite of the work involved, soon you will appreciate the sweet success of having your child potty trained.

CHAPTER 2. TOO YOUNG? TOO OLD?

Suggested Age for Potty Training

No less than one-three years old.

Potty training is an important turning point for kids. Most kids are prepared to start potty training between the ages of one year and one-and-a-half years. Regardless, a few kids will show signs of being prepared earlier or later than the normal age. All kids are unique and will have different experiences.

In opposition to the idea that a toddler isn't equipped to control his pee and poop until an older age, the study of child development shows that the sphincter muscles, which control bladder and bowel movements, start developing while the child is in utero and achieve their FULL maturity when the child is between 12 months and three years of age.

This is when toilet training ought to be COMPLETED, not begun.

When parents wait to begin potty training until AFTER these muscles achieve their full development, the muscles have actually been weakened by not having the regular use that takes place when a child learns toilet control.

It is our job as parents to react to the signs of readiness and give the opportunity for potty training at the earliest time possible.

You may begin seeing readiness signs at that age, when a lot of little children begin to demonstrate an enthusiasm for the potty chair or toilet. Pediatricians agree that most toddlers have a "window"' during which time it is easiest to potty train them.

For girls, this window is more often than not in the vicinity of two to two-and-a-half years of age, and for boys, around two-and-a-half to three, after which time children can develop a long-term habit of diaper use or can simply reject potty training.

Inexperienced parents may have the feeling that the earlier a toddler is acquainted with the potty, the longer the actual potty training will take, but that isn't actually the case. The best outcomes are for children who begin training between 19 months and two years of age. Normally, these kids are out of diapers by the time they reach 25 months.

Among children whose parents wait until they are around two and three years of age, some are trained quickly, but others take longer to train than those in the 19 month to two year window, partly because their potty training then coincides with the "terrible twos" period.

In the event that you see that your child is obviously not prepared to begin potty training, don't push him. There might be different issues going on that are causing him stress or causing his reluctance.

At the first sign of strong opposition to potty training from your toddler, you should hold off on potty training for around a month, and then try to approach potty training again without announcing it ahead of time.

In any case, as long as the child is willing, and the parents make the effort, they will be successful.

There is No One Particular Age to Start Potty Training

The transition from diapers to underwear will be much smoother if you look for signs of the child's readiness, as opposed to being settled on beginning at a particular age. Potty-training success relies on physical and emotional preparedness. It's up to us parents to understand this, and not to weigh down a child with a burden he isn't prepared for.

CHAPTER 3. HOW TO KNOW THE RIGHT TIME TO START

Do you remember the excitement of learning to ride a bike and being able to leave behind the tricycle? That gives a little bit of the idea of how it feels for a child to move from diapers to using the potty. There might be a period of time when it seems like it will never work, but it is exciting when it finally happens.

Within the window of time that tends to be best for potty training, every child will be different than others as to when he demonstrates readiness.

Younger siblings may take to the potty chair immediately if they are trying to copy an older sibling, or a child may be ready later because there is an upsetting event in the family around the same time that he would otherwise be ready.

But the most important thing is that you as a parent are able to tell when your child is READY.

Many parents have said more than once that they don't know how to tell when their child is ready for potty training. Here are a few of the typical signs to look for:

The Child Seems Interested in the Potty Chair or Toilet

✓ The child may get inspired by watching others use the toilet. (This may seem uncomfortable and awkward to begin with, but it is a decent way to show an example.)

✓ The child may watch you use the toilet, asking questions about the toilet or about sitting on the potty.

✓ The child shows enthusiasm for the toilet when another person is using it.

Global Readiness Skills, Apart from Showing Any Interest in the Toilet

✓ Able to walk and sit down without any help for brief timeframes.

✓ Can sit on and get up from a potty seat.

✓ Can balance himself with his feet so he can push when he's having a bowel movement.

Imitates His Parents Around the House

✓ Begins to demonstrate a desire to please parents or caregivers.

✓ Can return things to their place.

✓ Shows understanding of things having their place around the home.

✓ Is more autonomous with regards to completing tasks.

✓ Desires to be independent.

Has Dry Diapers for Up to Two Hours

✓ This demonstrates he's ready to store pee in his bladder.

✓ Must have the capacity to go to bed without a cup or glass.

✓ Has normal and formed bowel movements, even if bowel cycle is not yet regular.

Is Able to Communicate His or Her Wants

✓ Not necessarily through words yet, but through body movements, looks, hand gestures or other motions.

✓ Can comprehend and follow basic directions, for example, "Give the ball to Daddy."

✓ Understands words having to do with toileting.

✓ Tells you (or gives clear indications) when he poops or pees in his diaper or is going to.

It's vital for parents to figure out how their child communicates. It might start with physical discomfort, which transforms into wriggles and squirms, then little sounds and words, which is considered pre-language.

Is Uncomfortable with Wet or Soiled Diapers

✓ Complains about wet or dirty diapers, or does things like pulling off his diaper and peeing on the floor.

✓ Indicates that his or her diaper is wet or dirty. A toddler shows readiness for potty training when he is uncomfortable or awkward with having a wet diaper

✓ May make a request to be changed when the diaper is dirty or even try to remove the poop from his diaper.

✓ Starts to be aware that his diaper is going to be wet, looking down at it before he pees.

✓ Might make a request to wear clothing or to not put on a

diaper.

✓ May even have the capacity to pull down his pants and pull them up again with little help.

Not every one of these signs will necessarily be present when your toddler is ready for potty training. Most children show readiness with only a couple of these signs, but a general pattern of these types of signals will tell you it's a great time to begin.

Once more, if your child has as of late confronted or is going to confront a noteworthy change, for example, moving to a new house or the coming of another sibling, it is best to hold up briefly before really preparing. A little child who resists potty preparing today will be all the readier in another month.

Try not to feel forced to begin before your child signals readiness. Also, don't be influenced by anybody, regardless of whether they are parents, in-laws, friends, relatives or associates. If your child isn't ready to potty train, it isn't going to work.

Halfway measures just drag out the process of potty training, making it disappointing as opposed to fulfilling. Even as adults we realized that our digestive system and elimination can vary with our thoughts and feelings, and the same is true for a child. When the time is right, you can train your child with the three-day method, and he will figure out how to use the potty chair easily.

CHAPTER 4. PREPARING YOURSELF

Gardening and cooking shows on TV have a way of making what they do appear like it would be easy for us to achieve too. The colors look so appealing; everybody is rosy-cheeked and healthy, and completely calm with the culinary or gardening specialist.

The movements are so smooth, and in what seems like a matter of moments, the culinary specialist takes carrots from the perfect garden, whips up a carrot smoothie, and hands it to a waiting child, who tastes it and grins! How simple it all looks. We conclude that we need a garden like that, and we need to serve the same healthy food.

We imagine that we could plant the same vegetables and throw together the same healthy smoothies just like on TV. So, we go to the hardware store, buy some tools, and start digging up a spot for the garden. It doesn't take very long for us to realize that this project isn't going to be as simple as it looked. After a little bit of hard work with no immediate benefit, we lose interest and give up.

Many parents are like that when it comes to potty training. They eagerly anticipate potty training as a kind of "D-day" in their kid's development. The end of changing diapers is in sight! Unfortunately, many of these parents don't want to think about the amount of work it will take to potty train their kids. Who wants to think about that?

In reality, anything that is going to bring great enjoyment or benefit in the end has to be undertaken with attention and a certain amount of effort. We have to be prepared and ready to put some work into teaching our child the basics of potty training. Some toddlers get it within a couple of days. Some take a little longer. We should be ready to work with it for as long as it takes. I promise, it will be worth all the effort in the end, and won't take as long as you might think.

Here's a way that we shouldn't go about potty training, but one that happens all too often: we start potty training because we find out another child is on the way. Family and friends come from all around to shower us with love and concern, and while they are at it, they shower us with all kinds of advice as well. The fact that their own children can sometimes be little terrors, rather than the little angels they make them sound like, is a detail that sometimes gets left out of the advice.

Once we know another child is on the way, we start to think about getting our older child out of diapers, and the sooner the better. We start to wait anxiously for the appointed time. We're ready and we have all the necessary equipment ready. We have a picture in our minds of how potty training will go: a little drama, maybe some silliness, but most importantly a neat, happy ending.

On the designated day, we pull out the potty chair, almost expecting our child to applaud and grin when he sees it. Instead when he doesn't want the potty chair, pushes it away or cries when he sees it, we suddenly feel a great disappointment. We ask, "What did I do wrong?"

When the dust has settled, and we recover a little from the fact that our potty-training effort was a failure in spite of having it all planned out, we suddenly realize that we neglected the most important factor that needed to be considered: the child's readiness to be potty trained.

Potty training isn't just an event we can mark on the calendar like going camping, repainting the kitchen, or finishing up some work that someone else was supposed to do. When we prepare for the three days of potty training, the first people who need to be prepared are us, the parents, and one of the things we need to do is figure out how to see the signs that our toddler is about to poop or pee.

The actual potty training may only take three days, but we need to be committed to it for longer than that. Potty training is a part of the commitment we have to this little person that we brought into the world.

When you approach potty-training as one important part of your child's overall well-being, much the same as eating or sleeping, believe it or not, you can really relax. You can adopt a casual strategy to train your child. You don't need to stress. Being casual is something you can do to make your child's transition from diapers to the potty a peaceful process. You can relax once you:

✓ Let go of your desires.

✓ Stop comparing the child you are potty training with other kids, even with your other children.

✓ Know how your toddler's body and mind function.

✓ Recognize indications of readiness.

✓ Decide when and how to begin potty-training.

✓ Know how to discuss potty training with your child.

✓ Know what issues and difficulties to anticipate.

✓ Consider how you were potty-trained.

Be Involved in All Areas of Your Child's Learning

Before you bring out the potty chair, it helps a lot if you have already established an everyday routine with your child involving other areas of learning. When your child already has a daily routine, you can introduce the potty into the ordinary routine without it being a sudden huge change that could panic your child rather than intrigue him.

Children still need to recognize what is expected from them. If it happens that your child begins to move toward potty training intuitively or because he senses it is something you want from him, you can be a big help by providing guidance and praising his efforts, but always remember not to push him beyond his readiness.

A few children really are ready for potty training a lot earlier than others, so you aren't "pushing" your child if you aren't meeting any resistance.

But if there is resistance, that should be a sign your child isn't ready. At the same time, kids do love to learn to do things the way adults do them, so don't rob them of that chance if they are ready early.

Begin Potty Training Only When You and Your Child Are Ready

Your toddler may be ready for potty training, but how about you? Do you already have more on your schedule than you can deal with? Have you recently had another child? When you see that your child is ready, you need to also analyze whether you can devote the entire three days to helping your child figure out how to use the potty. You should be as ready as your toddler when you pick out the ideal time to put the three-day strategy in place.

Plan to Set Aside All Your Normal Activities for Three Whole Days

Try not to plan potty training for a time when you have a lot of other demands, like when you are moving to another house or expecting another child. It's best to wait until things have settled down and you have a regular schedule, so that both you and your child can have enough energy and cheerfulness to deal with setbacks and surprises.

Organize stand-ins or substitute help for day-to-day activities during those three days. But be sure to advise your relatives or friends who come to help you out that you won't be able to visit and chat with them like normal because you need to concentrate on the child that is being potty trained. It's vital that nothing distracts your attention, so that you can be available EVERY time your kid needs to poop or pee.

Choose three days when you have no other commitments, or reschedule any commitments you do have. A long weekend is perfect. If you do have other toddlers, find babysitters for them if you can, or plan to keep them busy with TV for the greater part of the day. Have meals ready ahead of time for those three days or have enough money ready for take-out food.

Decide on the Vocabulary

Make sure that all family members, long-term childcare providers or teachers use a similar routine with your child and use similar names for body parts and bathroom functions. Let them know about your process and ask them to use similar methods so that your child won't become confused.

Prepare to Dedicate Your Time and Energy to Your Child

You are ready to potty train when you are ready to give the time and energy needed to support your child in the process. Keep in mind that you may need to approach potty training your toddler differently that you did with your other kids, depending on how you read his signals and readiness.

Potty training boys is different from potty training girls. What's more, one little boy will be different than another as to how he responds to the training. Don't be surprised if potty training clicks quicker with one child or takes longer with another—that's just the way it is.

Try Not to Retreat to Diapers When the Going Gets Tough

Potty training is a process that is bound to have some setbacks and your child wetting himself is something he'll get over. You need to push on through the process with normal clothing and not fall back on training pants or pull-ups since that can end up actually confusing the child. For as long as the process takes, you can wipe up the pee or clean up the poop and know that it will click with them in the end.

Figure Out How Your Toddler Signals His Need to Pee or Poop

When you see signs that your child may need to use the potty, for example, facial gestures, squirming, hunching down or holding his crotch—react rapidly. Help your child to get comfortable with these signs, to stop what he is doing, and to make a beeline for the potty.

Praise your child for letting you know when he needs to go potty. When it's time to flush the toilet, let your child do the honors. Make sure that he washes his hands after using the potty.

Some parents try the technique of putting their child on the potty chair whether or not they have signaled a need to go. Or they may see that their child tends to have a bowel movement at a certain time and try putting him or her on the potty at that time.

This method doesn't work for all kids, and I for one am not

advocating it—genuine potty training starts when the child learns the feeling of needing to poop or pee and associates it with getting to the potty in time. So it is best to wait until the child actually needs to go in order to get him to use the potty.

If Possible, Don't Include Too Many People in the Actual Potty Training

If your spouse or a grandmother helps with potty training, make sure that you both use similar words and terms, so you don't confuse the child. But ideally, the parent who has seen the signs of readiness and has established a routine with the child should be the one to do the potty training.

If you are a nursing mother, you can still potty train your older child if you have worked into a normal routine with the new baby. Your toddler will normally be happy to help you with the baby, but at the time that he needs to go potty, stop nursing the infant and react to the needs of your toddler who is being potty trained.

At those moments when potty training seems particularly difficult, remember the inspiring motivations for the training that you are doing. You might need to remind yourself, "A couple of days of having to clean up several accidents is much better than a couple of years of dealing with stinky, dirty diapers."

CHAPTER 5. PREPARING THE CHILD

Apart from understanding the sensations of needing to go to the bathroom, getting there and taking clothes off, the toddler also needs to learn to first tighten their sphincter muscles to achieve control and then relax them to eliminate. It is a lot to learn. Gaining bowel and bladder control is a skill, but fortunately kids normally enjoy the chance to learn new skills.

The typical progression in learning these skills is that first comes bowel regularity, or having bowel movements at the same time, then bowel control.

Daytime bladder control usually follows, though for some toddlers it can happen at the same time as bowel control. Last of all comes nighttime bladder control.

Start to Teach Potty-Training Words

When you decide that the time has come to start potty training, there are a few things you can do to make the change from diapers to underwear smoother. Instruct your child a few words related to going to the potty, for instance, you might need to teach him words like "pee," "poop" and "I have to go."

Before actually starting potty training, begin reacting to your child's dirty diapers with words that express the idea that it is yucky to poop in a diaper. Be clear about this. Talk them through the process of going to the potty over and over (pulling down pants, sitting, pooping or peeing, pulling up the pants, washing hands). Make it ordinary.

Begin to Make Diaper-changing Tedious

Once your child starts to show discomfort with a dirty diaper, try to start making changing his diaper as much of an inconvenience for him as it is for you, so that using the potty will seem less demanding by comparison. Start to show your kid what normal (non-padded) underwear looks like. If you are using cloth diapers, this step isn't as essential because your child will understand and become uncomfortable with the feeling of a wet or dirty diaper much sooner.

A child who is always kept in disposable diapers won't learn to stay dry because he doesn't have the chance to feel wet. Once he stops wearing disposables and starts wearing underwear, it will take a while for him to start understanding and disliking the feeling of being wet, and for him to learn to sense those feelings before peeing.

Acquaint Your Toddler with the Bathroom

Two or three weeks before beginning the actual three-day potty training, start taking your child with you into the bathroom with the goal that he will feel comfortable in the bathroom. You might keep a fun potty-training book or an interesting new toy in the bathroom for him to use while sitting on the potty seat. Stay with your toddler when he is in the bathroom, even if he stays a long time, and praise him for even trying to use the potty chair.

Let your child watch other people who are using the toilet and talk about what they're doing. Talk about how they use the toilet paper and how they use new tissue paper for each wipe.

Give your child a chance to work on flushing the toilet. When you're done using the toilet, have your toddler flush it for you, waving bye-bye to the poop. Let him see pee and poop in the toilet and let him practice flushing it.

Present the Potty Chair

It's good to make the potty chair available to your toddler early on, so that he definitely knows what it's for before you begin the actual three-day training. It will be a lot less demanding for your child, if for a long time previous to the training, you have mentioned the potty chair and he is familiar with it, as opposed to introducing it to him right at the time you begin the training.

It's also good to put the potty chair in the bathroom, not just anywhere in the house like in the child's bedroom or playroom, or somewhere in the yard. In a multi-story house, put the potty chair in the bathroom where your toddler will typically use it during the day.

It's good to start to demonstrate using the potty chair by having your toddler sit on it even before he is prepared and begins to go potty in it. You can encourage him to sit on the potty chair with or without a diaper. Make sure that his feet reach the floor comfortably or place something under his feet so that they will reach comfortably. Teach your child how to talk about using the bathroom using simple, basic terms. You might even dump the contents of his dirty diaper into the potty chair to demonstrate its purpose.

Make Your Child's Potty a Comfortable and Welcoming Place

One week before the real three-day potty-training process, make sure that the potty chair is in a well-lit bathroom that is accessible to your toddler. The potty should be a welcoming place. Let your toddler look, handle and get comfortable with the potty chair. Tell him that this potty chair is his own special chair. Present it to him and discuss it, letting him try it out and get comfortable with it.

Encourage your child to use his potty chair whenever he

needs to go poop or pee. Tell him that he can let you know any time he needs to go and that you will be available to take him to the bathroom at any time.

In the event your child is reluctant or hesitant to use the potty chair, don't push the issue. Maybe you have planned on starting potty training but then some stressful matters have come up, interfering with your carefully laid plans. If you try to potty train anyway, the potty-training time will be tense and rushed rather than casual and relaxed. If something comes up to interfere with your plans, reschedule the three-day block of time, and your child will regain interest when things are no longer stressful.

Schedule Potty Breaks

In the two weeks leading up to the actual three-day potty training, set your child on the potty chair when you think he will need to pee or poop. There might be a pattern you've noticed, like going about 30 minutes after eating or right after bathing. But these are just guides. Don't take him to the potty if he isn't showing any signs at all of needing to go.

You can show your toddler where his bowel movements go even while he is still wearing diapers before the actual training begins. Show him how the potty chair is used. Whenever he poops in his diaper, take him to the potty chair, sit him down, and dump the diaper into the potty chair. This will help him make the association between sitting on the potty chair and pooping, and will help him to understand the purpose of the potty chair.

Once you have dumped the potty chair into the bathroom toilet, you can let your child flush to see where excrement goes (of course don't make him do it if he is afraid of the toilet). It's not as helpful to have the toddler sit on the potty chair fully dressed if the goal is for him to make the association between the bodily functions and the chair. For little boys, it's normal for them to start out sitting on the potty chair to go pee as well, and then later learn to go standing up after potty training is finished, usually when they want to copy their father or older brothers.

Experience has shown that it doesn't do a lot of good to set your child on the potty chair when he doesn't need to go. It's best not to make your toddler sit on the potty for long periods of time because it will then feel like a punishment rather than a relief.

Put a low step or stool by the bathroom sink so that your child can reach the faucet to wash his hands. Teach him how to wash his hands after using the potty. Make it a pattern to ask him if he has washed his hands and to guide him using soap and water as you talk him through the process. This can be a fun activity that your child enjoys as part of his normal routine.

CHAPTER 6. POTTY-TRAINING CALENDAR

Designate Three Days in a Row

Mark them on your calendar. Keep in mind that the three days shouldn't be sandwiched between big events or occasions that require a lot of work and attention. Unless you can get extra time off from work, the best time is usually a three-day weekend like Labor Day or Memorial Day.

During these three days, don't plan on going anywhere. You need to allow yourself to focus on the potty training because consistency is the way to achieve the goal. Plan ahead for how regular errands can be taken care of during those days. If your child is normally in childcare, reschedule so that he is at home the whole time.

Set Up a Variety of Activities You and Your Toddler Can Do Together

You can plan some activities outside in the yard during the three days of potty training, keeping in mind that you need to be able to rush into the potty frequently, but it's best to mostly plan on being inside. In the house, try to spend most of your time in an area that has an easy-to-clean floor. Prepare yourself with books, colored pencils, markers, playdough, puzzles, toys and TV shows. You need to keep your child occupied and cheerful during this three-day process, and three days inside with a toddler takes a certain amount of creativity.

Have Your Laundry Done Before Starting

You need to have clean sheets, extra jammies and clothes

ready in case your child has an accident once the training starts.

Introduce High-fiber Foods to Your Child's Diet

High-fiber foods help avoid constipation by keeping enough liquid in the stools, making the stool soft and easy to eliminate.

Offer a high-fiber, simple-to-eat grain as a main ingredient of your child's daily meals. Most toddlers will cheerfully eat oats that are high in fiber.

For supper, serve yogurt with added fiber. Toddlers love yogurt, and those with extra fiber in them are just as tasty and have the same smooth texture as other yogurts.

Make sandwiches on high-fiber wheat bread. Try serving your child nut butter and jam on high-fiber wheat bread or on whole-grain white bread. A white bread including whole grain doesn't have as much fiber as 100 percent whole wheat, but it certainly provides more fiber than traditional white bread.

Include high-fiber vegetables like broccoli, sweet potatoes, spinach and cabbage as an interesting part of your toddler's meals. You can serve sweet potatoes with a little butter and brown sugar, or include some spinach or shredded cabbage on a turkey sandwich.

Foods like beans, sweet potatoes, peas, tomatoes, and corn are all very high in fiber. Cook a sweet potato in the microwave for five to seven minutes. Peel it, then cut it into circles with a mold or cookie cutter, and serve it. Serve steamed green beans or cauliflower with ranch dressing for dipping. Mashed peas out of the fridge are a nice, cool treat on a late spring day.

Offer high-fiber fruits, like apples, pears, and prunes to your little child every day. Natural products are an easy approach to add fiber to your little child's eating routine. Serve fruits and vegetables with the peel when possible, because the skin has a higher fiber content. Prunes and apricots have a great laxative effect, as well as being high in fiber.

Cut grapes or cherry tomatoes in half and serve them with whole grain crackers. Core an apple and spread a thin layer of nut butter on apple slices. Avocados are high in fiber and are a soft and tasty treat for younger children. For variety, you might want to serve an assortment of cut-up fruits and veggies on a brightly-colored plate or even in an ice cube tray.

Serve your toddler whole grain pasta and brown rice instead of their highly-refined white counterparts.

Nutritionists suggest cutting back cheese and other dairy products in your toddler's diet during the potty-training period since they can have a constipating effect. Also, offer your child a lot of water, which will help prevent constipation and will keep that bladder full, giving your little one lots of chances to practice!

A diet rich in high-fiber foods will not only make potty training easier for you and your toddler, it's also a great way to present healthy foods to your toddler and establish a pattern of eating healthily from an early age.

CHAPTER 7. EQUIPMENT ARSENAL

Have all the needed supplies ready before you begin the real three days of potty training.

High-fiber Food Supplies and Fluids

You should have more liquids on hand than your child typically drinks in a day. Water is ideal. Besides water, an assortment of natural fruit juices is also good.

Potty Chair

Take your child with you to shop for the potty chair and let him pick out one he likes. It is best to start with a potty chair which sits on the floor and later, if you want, you can move to one that sits on the toilet seat of a normal toilet.

You can take the potty chair with you, even when you are out and about. Kids become comfortable with their potty chair and some prefer it over a public toilet when away from home. Try to figure out what works best for your toddler and go with it. In the end, your toddler will figure out how to use both his potty chair and the toilet.

Take your child to the store with you, let him sit on various potty chairs if possible, and let him pick out the one he wants. As much as he can, allow him to help you take it out of the store, put it in the car, and set it up in the bathroom when you get home.

Real Underwear

You should have 10 to 20 pairs on hand. Take your child

with you to pick out some "big boy" underwear. Stay away from padded underwear or pull-ups. As a way of working up enthusiasm on the part of your toddler, take him on a shopping trip a week before the actual three-day training time, and let him pick out a couple of packs of underwear. A lot of times a toddler will get excited about using "big boy" underwear with his favorite cartoon character on them.

The three-day strategy for potty training moves straight from diapers to regular clothes and underwear, with no pull-ups or training pants as a potty-training aid, since wearing pull-ups actually encourages kids to pee in them. Disposable training pants are advertised as a gentle introduction to normal underwear, but they aren't really effective.

Training pants may seem to be helpful at first since they keep you from having to deal with a mess on your floors, couches and other furniture, but they actually confuse toddlers and make them think it is okay to use them like diapers. For that reason, using training pants often works against potty-training progress.

Pull-ups are another item that actually delays potty-training progress. They have for some time been criticized because they keep the child from feeling wetness from accidents, thus slowing down the learning process. Sadly, they are regularly advertised for use as underwear for three and four year-olds who are not yet potty trained, which further puts off developing the skills of controlling bodily functions.

Easy-wear Clothing

Make sure your child's wardrobe is suitable for potty training. Try to avoid overalls or clothes with buttons and snaps. Simple clothes that allow the child to easily undress himself are essential at this stage of potty training.

Moist Baby Wipes

You can keep wet wipes in the bathroom for a few days ahead of time so your toddler knows that they are for him to use. Wet wipes offer a cleaner and more delicate wipe than toilet paper, but most baby wipes and other wet wipes are not made of biodegradable material and can't be flushed down the toilet because they don't disintegrate. There are some flushable wet wipes available, but some of them contain household cleaning agents that can be aggravating if they contact the eyes.

There are also economical ways to make your own wet wipes. A lot of mothers have learned how to make two rolls of wet wipes out of one roll of paper towels by cutting it in half and soaking the halves in a mixture of water, baby soap and baby oil or almond oil. Then the wipes are stored in an air and water-proof container and remain moist for a month or two. When you look at the cost, it makes a lot of sense, and you can customize the scent.

Others make their own homemade reusable baby wipes out of cloth. Though that may sound gross to those who are used to using disposable wipes, it definitely saves money and is much better for the environment. Making reusable baby wipes from the best available material will cost less than $60 for a set of 24 cloths that will last you from birth to potty training. Traditional wipes tend to cost about $4 for a pack of 80, which might last only seven days, running up a total cost of $208 every year!

When you make your own baby wipes, you know exactly what is in the soap solution, so you know exactly what is touching your child's skin. Instead of the alcohol, fragrance and chlorine normally found in traditional baby wipes, custom-made wipes can be made with entirely safe substances and paper towels. Homemade wipes are durable and are the least aggravating to your toddler's skin.

Snacks, Treats and Rewards

Come up with a reward system that matches your parenting style and doesn't conflict with what your toddler is used to from you. For instance, you might buy a gift bag with your toddler's favorite cartoon character and fill it with "pee prizes" or "poop prizes." Coloring books, small toys and individual Hershey's Kisses are examples of some of these rewards. Or you could let your toddler pick a prize when he goes poop and use stickers and fruit snacks when he goes pee.

For some parents, M&M's Minis are a big help in potty training. Each time your child goes potty, he gets a few, but if he wipes himself (which is a tremendous accomplishment), he is rewarded with four or five pieces of chocolate.

This helps a toddler to overcome the difficulty of not wanting to poop on the potty because learning how to wipe himself is yucky.

If your child reacts well to stickers or stars on a chart, you could use that method too. A reward chart can be a useful tool to use so the toddler can see a visual indication of how well he is progressing. Some parents reward their child with a new book, toy, or other gifts when he has stayed dry or used the potty for a certain amount of time.

For others, trips to the park or an extra bedtime story are effective rewards. Figure out what works best for your child. Reinforce your child's efforts with verbal praise, for example, "You're doing great! You're learning how to use the potty just like big kids do!" Even if your toddler doesn't do everything successfully, give praise for any part of the procedure that he can do.

Cleaning Supplies

You will also need to have supplies on hand for cleaning up accidents; for example, cleaning rags, soap or disinfectant, and a plastic bucket.

CHAPTER 8. THREE-DAY POTTY-TRAINING METHOD

The Rule that Makes the Three-Day Method Effective

Each child is different. Even among siblings, each child will show different signs of readiness, react differently to training, and learn in his or her own particular way, which then should be encouraged. But just because things don't seem to be working at first the way we expected, that doesn't mean that "the technique doesn't work" and that you should throw out the whole strategy.

This is one reason to read through this book a few times BEFORE starting the Three-Day technique, and not while you're in the middle of it. After you give it a while to stew in your mind as you watch your toddler's reactions and disposition, by the time you start the three-day training, you will know the concepts "by heart" and won't simply have to go "by the book."

Once you read through this material a few times, you'll know how to personalize the ideas in the three-day technique. You will be able to know in what areas to be flexible and in what areas to be firm and consistent. For example, you may change ideas about what kind of prizes to use and how, but will know that you must be firm about using normal clothes and not pull-ups after you get rid of the diapers.

At the very center of what is firm and what is flexible, there are certain principles that make the three-day potty-training technique effective. They apply to every child, without much variation because of the kid's personality. Be prepared to never fall short in the areas of:

Persistence

Consistency

Patience

Positivity

Love

No Discipline, Punishment, or Negative Correction strategies

Accidents are going to happen, so be ready for them. Even children who have used the potty effectively for a long time sometimes have accidents. Try not to make your child feel bad for having an accident. Scolding your child will actually make the potty-training process take longer, not less time. Keep this in mind when you feel frustrated.

Instead of scolding your toddler, remind him to let you know when he needs to go potty so you can take him right away. Keep in mind that encouragement is the most effective strategy, so keep praising your toddler for a job well done or for trying.

There are some occasions when a child who won't go on the potty will poop or pee immediately if a diaper is put back on. Don't be discouraged. In spite of the fact that it is tempting to return to diapers or pull-ups, keep using normal clothing, even in nighttime training. In the end it will be worth all the effort.

Getting your toddler ready ahead of time will definitely help, which is why it is good to help your toddler get acquainted with the potty for the two weeks prior to starting the actual training.

And even if you are a parent or caregiver who has physical limitations that keep you from participating in some aspects of potty training, you can definitely still be involved in the teaching, rewarding, and other non-physical parts of the process.

TRAINING DAY 1

Your Preparation

Training day 1 should start with you being mentally prepared and feeling positive. It is wise to be up and dressed before your little one is, perhaps even have the first coffee or get a couple of little tasks out of the way.

For the next three days, your job is to remember that accidents are going to happen, and maybe even after the three days. This is perfectly normal. Under no circumstances should you tell your child off or punish them. Accept the fact that you may have a little extra washing but never get angry or lose your patience. It will only make potty training last longer.

While enjoying this moment of peace and mental preparation, remember that day 1 will be the hardest, and you are going to have to dedicate more time to your son. This is why, if you are a working mom, it is best to start on a day of the week when you have fewer other responsibilities. Don't laugh but knowing that the system was so effective, I saved one of my holiday days and took a Friday off work so that I could devote my attention to my second son.

Getting Dressed

When your little lad gets up on training day 1, they need to be reminded that today is a special day and that there are no more diapers. Use sentences like, "you're such a big boy." Have them dressed in new underwear and make sure you are making a big deal of the underwear.

At this point, some moms will go straight for the amazing superhero underwear. I can understand this, but the chances of accidents today are high. I prefer not to bring out the extra special underwear on day 1 because I don't want them to be upset when there is an accident. So, for day 1, a value pack, cheap underwear is the best underwear in the world, or at least that's what my son believes.

Again, there are parents who prefer to go bottomless, which is another option. I have used underwear for all three of mine because it made more sense to get them used to pulling them down and up. I have never been one for pull up diapers because it provides the sensation of a regular diaper and won't help the child remember to use the potty.

All of your little boy's clothes should be loose and easy to take off. If it is cold, but you don't want him to wear trousers, big thick socks or leg warmers are an excellent replacement. As you are getting him dressed, talk about what a special day it is and how he is going to be using the potty, or even the big boy potty, today.

At the same time, it is necessary for your son to know that he has to tell you when he needs to use the potty. As a mom, choose your vocabulary and stick with the same words or phrases:

- "Do you need to go for a wee/poo?"

- "Do you need to pee/poo?"

- "Do you need to go to the potty?"

- "Do you want to use the potty?"

Choose one and stick to it so that your child associates that phrase with going to the potty.

Having Breakfast

High fiber is the key to firm stools. Whole grain cereals, whole grain bread, pears, bananas, and yogurt is high in fiber. It's a special day so don't go punishing the poor thing with a bowl of all bran and whole-grain toast if they don't like it. If you have a fussy eater, try hiding some high fiber food in their favorite breakfast.

You will also want to make sure you get a big class of fluid in them with their breakfast. Fruit juice is better than milk because of the fiber. If you have time, try making a nice high in fiber smoothie that can be drunk throughout the day.

Throughout the Day

From here on out, you will need to spend the entire day with a watchful eye on your son. Any signs of going to the bathroom and you quickly take them straight to the potty. Every 15 to 20 minutes, without fail, you need to ask your child if they need to use the potty.

Start healthy habits from day one and encourage your child to wash their hands after every potty trip. You can begin to see why you need to have a relatively free day, as between multiple trips to the bathroom, hand washing, and cleaning after possible accidents, there won't be much time for anything else.

Naptime

Naturally, naptime and bedtime are going to be more difficult. Put your child on the potty before the nap and immediately after waking up. If they do wet the bed, do not get angry or frustrated. Let them know that it's not a problem and accidents happen when we are learning new things.

Afternoon and Dinner

If you don't have to go out, don't feel the need to. Some fresh air is great, but it is more important that on day 1 to be as close to the potty and your child is able to go as soon as they feel the need.

I have always tried to make the most of this day together. Get the paints out or do a puzzle. Read some books and have a cuddle while you watch their favorite cartoon together. Use each activity as a chance to put your child on the potty. So, after you clean up toys, try the potty before having a snack, for example. Although it might be difficult for you not to try and achieve multiple tasks, this is your task today.

As with breakfast, make sure there is a strong element of fiber in their meals and plenty of fluids. With my second child, we had a celebratory dinner after day 1. This will provide family time for other members to join in with the day's achievements. Also, don't forget to sit them on the potty before and after lunch and dinner, and wash hands.

Bedtime

For some parents, we are amazed at how naturally easy bedtime training can be and your child picks it up very quickly. For others, it may take longer than three days. Remember, each child is different, so this is fine. Don't get upset if your child doesn't stay dry throughout the night straightaway. Have a mattress protector (you will need a spare one), a few sets of sheets, and some patience.

What About the Poo?

With such frequent trips to the potty, you would hope that

on one or two of these occasions, your child poops. If not, you should make sure that you put them on the potty at the time of the day they would have pooped in a diaper. So, if you know your child poops around 30 minutes after waking up, make sure there is a potty trip at this time.

Possible Issues on Training Day 1

Not Enough or Too Much Time on the Potty

I can laugh now but I remember my eldest son sitting on the potty for maybe 10 seconds and saying no. Then about two minutes later, we had a little accident. You almost feel like they are doing it on purpose, but they really aren't.

It is recommended that toddlers spend 3-5 minutes on the potty. You may need to let them take a book to read in order to relax. Don't take toys because this shouldn't be associated with playtime and obviously, the concerns for hygiene.

The problem with spending too much time on the potty is that your child may start to feel like it's a punishment. This weekend you have dedicated time to potty training, but you don't want them to spend 20 minutes in the bathroom each time—for one, you won't have time for this, and two, there will be time for this when they are teenagers.

Your Child Refuses to Go to the Potty

There might come a point when they are a little fed up with constantly going to the bathroom. If this is the case, tell them in advance when the potty trip is coming up. Use simple phrases like, "before we have lunch, we will try and use the potty" or "after we play with the cars, we will try and use the potty."

If you see that your child isn't keen to use the bathroom. You need to up your game with the positive reinforcement, whether that's through praise or prizes.

The End of Training Day 1

You have made it! You have survived the hardest day. Your washing machine might be overloaded, you might have the sensation that you are still covered in pee. You might feel like you have failed or that you have conquered the world.

Don't think that positive reinforcement is only for the kids! Crack open the bottle of chardonnay, peel back the lid of those chocolates and reward yourself. Even if there have been accidents, and you don't feel it has gone as well as you had expected, you will have achieved more today than you realize, so take a moment to celebrate that.

TRAINING DAY 2

What few of the other books and blogs will tell you about the 3-day process is how much of the success depends on the attitude of the mom (or parent). This is something that stuck me on the morning of training day 2 with my second son.

The success of day 2 will greatly depend on the results of

day 1—if you are not careful. Between my own experience and talking to other parents, 7 am (or 8 am/9 am if you are lucky) on day 2 is probably more important than day 1. This is the time you need to prepare yourself.

Imagine day 1 went amazingly well. In your mind, you have no doubt that day 2 is going to be even better as logically, your son will have learned from day 1. Second scenario is that day 1 was horrendous, and so you are only expecting another day swimming in pee. In reality, every day our little ones surprise us with the good and the bad that they do. Potty training is no different.

Day 2 should start the same way as day 1 for you. It's important that you take the time to have those few minutes of peace to prepare yourself. Yesterday, whether good or bad, is in the past and today is going to be a good day. It is crucial that you remember not to get angry, not to lose your patience and never punish if there is an accident.

Getting Dressed

Now that your son is aware of what to do on the potty, the absolute first thing to do is to take him to sit on the potty using the same vocabulary as you chose the day before, literally "Good morning darling. Do you need a wee?"

If your child has wet the bed, he has to know that this is not a problem. Here, I try to remind people that it's not just the words that you say. Children are very intuitive and will pick up on facial expressions and body language. Speaking through gritted teeth or even smiling like a Cheshire Cat will contradict your words.

Once the first potty trip is out of the way, the day should start with the same positive attitude as the previous day. He is such a big boy, and he is doing so well using the big boy potty. I would still hold off on the superhero underwear, even if yesterday was accident-free. What I would do is ask if he wants to choose his underwear. It works as a sign of faith and as a reward.

If you chose the bottomless option for day 1, you should select some loose fitted trousers for day 2, and this is recommended even if you don't feel you made the right progress on day 1. Your child will have grasped the concept of using the potty, if not the practice. Trousers are important to establish a routine and learn to pull them up and down. Not putting them on may save you washing but it won't help your child learn.

Even if it has only been 20 minutes or half an hour, ask your son again if he needs to use the potty after getting dressed. I know you have just pulled up the trousers and it would make more sense to ask before putting the trousers on, but day 2 still requires regular asking.

Mealtimes and Snacks

Breakfast, in particular, should be similar to day 1. Look for foods that are high in fiber. I am a fan of milk for breakfast, so I love treating mine to warm milk and high-fiber biscuits to dunk. Fruit juice is a great choice too. Have faith in what is right for your child.

I also like using mealtimes as rewards for these three days. Now that I have dedicated time to the potty-training process, I try to make the most of every moment. Cooking with children is messy so while the washing machine is "earning its keep," there is no harm in cooking with the kids and throwing a few more items in.

The best thing about cooking with your kids is that you can sneak in those ingredients that they might turn their noses up at. Pizza is probably the perfect example. If you make your own pizza base, you can add whole wheat flour, which is higher in fiber and even spread some flaxseed. Also, you can select fresh vegetables of your choice for more vitamins and minerals. Make it fun and create pizza faces.

Some will recommend having salty snacks available. On the one hand, it will increase the amount of fluid intake. On the other hand, salty snacks may lead to bad eating habits in the future.

It is recommended that toddlers should have a daily salt intake of 2g. Personally, I feel that a little bit of everything is OK so if you feel you need to increase your child's fluid intake, try savory biscuits or popcorn.

In terms of the potty, make sure you sit your little man on the potty before and after meals and continue with the healthy habit of hand washing.

Throughout the Day

If your child is showing signs of wanting to go to the potty alone, this is great and probably a sign that you can reduce the number of times you need to keep asking. I start the day by asking every 20 to 30 minutes, and if it looks like we are going in the right direction, reduce it to maybe every hour if they are asking to go by themselves.

If necessary, keep asking the question of the three days until you feel it's the right time to become less persistent. Nevertheless, on day 2, you should still be taking your child before and after meals and naptimes.

Naptime and Bedtime

There are no special tips or tricks for this time of the day. It will be very similar to day 1. Make sure you take your child to use the potty before and after having a nap and before going to bed. Let them know that even if they have had an accident, they are doing a great job.

Even though they aren't showing it, little boys may be upset or frustrated by accidents. Take advantage of naptime and bedtime for hugs, kisses and love to fill them with confidence.

What about the poop?

Hopefully today your son will poop on the potty. If this isn't the case, don't worry. Make an effort to praise the living daylights out of getting that one step closer. You should still be taking your child to the potty around the same time of day as they would poop in a diaper.

Can We Go Out?

Yes! Day 2 of training is when you can take a walk or run some errands, but it is still wise to keep this trip to around 20 minutes. Obviously, there should be a potty trip before you go out and as soon as you come home. I always try to make sure we go out once they have had a poop, just to be on the safe side.

Possible Issues on Training Day 2

Your Child Seems to Have Made No Progress

As the problem suggests, it seems that your child has made no progress. It doesn't mean they haven't. This new routine may take a little longer for some to grasp. This is not a sign that the three-day progress doesn't work.

Go back to the positive reinforcement and come up with a plan that is more motivating for your child. My sons loved stickers; my daughter was thrilled with a pen. Think outside the box. Remember that positive reinforcement isn't spoiling them. It is showing them how well they are doing.

Rewards may not be what your child needs and perhaps it's your praise they need to hear. When I say get excited that your son uses the potty, I really do mean get excited. I'm talking about dancing like it's 1999 for even just a drop of pee.

You are Losing Your Motivation

Don't assume this is limited to first-time moms. I know people who have had the easiest 3-day potty training program with two or even three children and for some reason, the next time feels the complete opposite.

Also, don't assume that you are not allowed to have this moment of self-doubt. However, burn this into your mind— it's a moment. Pick yourself up and know that this is a phase just like sleepless nights, the terrible twos and the hormonal years.

You grew a human inside you for nine months, you gave life to a human, you can potty train. At the end of day 2, you reward yourself for your efforts and go to bed knowing that tomorrow is a new day.

If you need to, take a break. Leave the kids with someone else and get out of the house for a while. A little bit of alone time might be all you need to recharge your batteries.

TRAINING DAY 3

Rather than repeat a lot of the information from day 1 and day 2, let's take a look at some of the routines and habits from the first two potty-training days that should be maintained for day 3:

• You will still need a significant time to spend with your little one, so try not to plan anything.

- A high fiber diet with plenty of fluids. Your child should have access to water throughout the entire day and more so during the 3-day potty training program.

- Loose fitted clothing and trousers that are easy to pull up and down. You may have noticed by now that long T-shirts are a nuisance because they can't see around them to the trousers.

- There shouldn't be any use of diapers or pull up pants. Don't succumb to this because it will undo the mental preparation you have been working on. Even if you aren't seeing the results, your child's brain now knows that it has to send a "potty signal."

- Before and after meals and naptimes, you should be taking your child to use the potty and wash hands. For the rest of the day, you may still need to ask if they need to use the potty but not as frequently as the previous days.

- Regardless of your child's progress, there is still to be no loss of patience or temper. As well as this, your positivity will have to be just as enthusiastic as the previous days, especially if they are achieving greater things.

It doesn't take a psychologist to tell you that day 3 is going to depend on day 2 in terms of your mentality and perspective. But there is no point in making negative assumptions because day three is often the day that toddlers seem to just get it.

You may wake up to a dry bed or your little one may wake

up and ask to go to the potty. This is truly fantastic and should be celebrated. If you feel like day 2 had positive results and you have had a dry night, it might be a good time to get the superhero underwear out.

Instead of thinking that this is the last day and trying to put more emphasis on everything, keep doing what you have been doing. Start your day with your usual routine and a few minutes to process the plan. If you are feeling nervous or stressed, find a way to unwind before the kids are up.

My Top Tips for a Five Minute De-stress

• Take long, deep breaths, focus on inhaling and exhaling. The additional oxygen works wonders.

• Read something unrelated to potty training—do not Google what you are doing wrong.

• Meditate, if you have no idea where to begin, use an app.

• Stretching increases blood flow and makes you feel re-energized.

• Put on your favorite songs and dance it out. I find this more effective when you are alone.

• Write a to-do list. It might be activities you want to do that day or long-term goals.

If you are a working mom, I would start with the to-do list. When we spend a significant amount of time away from work it is almost like we forget that we have successful careers. Our usual coffee breaks have become five-minute potty breaks. More often than not, a quick to-do list will remind you of your other responsibilities.

This is not to say that you should feel guilty about taking the time for the 3-day potty training program. What you are doing now is just as valuable, if not more, than preparing the next quarterly budget. Creating a to-do list reminded me that this is just a phase and that soon, I would be back in the office. If anything, it motivated me more to spend this entire day with my son.

When you take your child from their bed and there has been an accident, make sure he knows that it is absolutely fine and it's not a problem.

Stick to the same routine of going straight to the potty and then getting dressed in loose fitted clothing. If there has been no bed wetting make a huge deal of this, allow for a special celebratory breakfast and even consider phoning a family member to share the good news.

What Should You Do If Your Son Needs More Assistance on Training Day 3?

Thanks to the Internet, there are an array of books and videos aimed at helping young children learn to use the potty. If you haven't already, it might be wise to take advantage of some of these now.

If you don't feel that the right progress has been made on day 1 and 2, it still doesn't mean that it isn't working or that you should go back to diapers. Instead, try one of the following resources after breakfast:

- Sesame Street Video - Potty Time

- Pirate Pete's Potty - Potty Training Video for Toddlers

- CoComelon Nursery Rhymes - Potty Training Song

- Leslie Patricelli - Potty Book

You can find plenty of themed stories, songs and videos, so you will be able to find something that will appeal to your son's interests.

Leaving the House

By day 3, you should be able to safely leave the house for up to an hour, ensuring that you sit your son on the potty before you leave and as soon as you get home again.

Take spare clothes just in case. If there is an accident, really emphasize that it's OK. Your son might feel more embarrassed because you are out and about.

Even if there is an accident, try going out again in the afternoon for another 30 minutes to an hour. The trick is to pay close attention to the morning trip out so as not to repeat the same pattern.

So, if your son wet himself five minutes before getting home, shorten the trip to 45 minutes.

Possible Issues on Training Day 3

You Feel Like There Are Still Too Many Accidents or Close Calls

As parents, we often forget that even on day 3, toddlers still need frequent reminding. This won't be as often as day 1, but you still need to ask them if they need to go to the potty and even take them if they haven't been for a while.

The most common cause of accidents at this stage is that they are just completely engrossed in what they are doing and forget to go to the potty. This is likely to be when they are playing or watching TV. When your child is focused on an activity for a long time, don't forget to ask them.

Day 3 is usually the day when you see the most results, especially if you have followed the guidelines of the program. Your little champion has accomplished a lot in a short time and needs to be praised for his efforts, as do you. At the end of day 2, make sure there is something special for the whole family at the end of this day.

Even if your child is potty trained, there might still be the odd accident, and this is perfectly normal. Don't forget to tell other caregivers and daycare staff the progress you have made and the key vocabulary you have been using.

If your son isn't completely potty trained, it just means they need a day or two more to master the skills. It could be that tomorrow you wake up and the penny just drops. Don't give up and keep being patient.

CHAPTER 9. WHAT IF YOU DON'T HAVE 3 DAYS

Let's face it, with all that we have going on and all the things we need to get done, we may have too many responsibilities to dedicate three whole days. While the 3-day program is optimal and achieves the best results, due to work commitments, you may only have two days to complete the process.

If you need to potty train your child in just two days, again, you will have to be aware of the signs that they are ready. It is also recommended to wait a little longer. Two-day training needs more daytime bladder control, which is likely to come in at around the age of two, sometimes even three when the bladder muscles are stronger.

Rather than having a clean diaper for a couple of hours, you will want to see a clean diaper for several hours, which is another reason why it is better to wait for a couple of months compared with the 3-day training program.

You may have already been talking about the potty with your child by now and have a potty in the bathroom. In some cases, young boys are not motivated to use it, and we find ourselves having to change the tactics.

The 3-day program was all about key vocabulary to use the potty. If you want to achieve the same results but in two days, it's all about keeping the special underwear clean. As the child is slightly older, they will have a better understanding of looking after what is theirs.

Preparation for the 2-Day Potty Training Program

Now that the objective is all about keeping their underwear clean and dry, you need to show that you trust they can do this. For this program, it is worth starting out on the first morning with the special underwear. Before you begin, have a special shopping trip and let them choose the underwear they want—regardless of your opinions.

On the same shopping trip, you might want to invest in a bathroom buddy. This shouldn't be a new toy, rather a doll or a figure that is close by and goes to the bathroom to use the potty with them. Having a toy that is associated with the potty will remind them to go. Don't let him sit on the potty for too long and play, and limit potty time to 3-5 minutes.

You will also need small treats that can be used for positive reinforcements, little sweets, stickers, anything that they find amazing.

Mealtimes and Naptimes

Breakfast, lunch and dinner will be the same as for the 3-day program. Keep meals and snacks high in fiber and plenty of fruit juice. They should have water available throughout the whole day.

Still don't be tempted to put diapers on for naps or bedtime. You child needs to feel when their underwear is wet, and their brains won't send the right messages if they have diapers or pull-up training pants on.

Throughout the Day

This is an intense version of the 3-day program so day 1 should still be predominantly at home, close to the potty, if possible. Begin the day by explaining what a special day it is and that they will be using the potty. Start by going straight to the potty and ask every 20 minutes if they need to go.

By the afternoon, your little one might be showing you signs that he needs to go to the potty, and you can begin to ask less often. It's a case of playing it by ear and reading the signs of your son. If you feel like he is making good progress, you could go for a short walk in the afternoon.

Overcoming Problems with the 2-Day Potty Training Program

You can lead a horse to water, but you can't make it drink. Trying to force the process won't help. The most important thing is that you are consistent; consistent with asking if they need to use the potty, consistent with your praise and with your patience.

Some children will pick it up by day one, others on day two. There will be children who need a little more time, so you need to stick to the plan and remember that each child is different. Even moms with multiple children are amazed that the exact same process can have different results for each of their children.

This is a huge milestone for your son and getting it right from the beginning will make your life easier and do wonders for their confidence. Enjoy the process, which I know sounds ironic because there will probably be plenty of cleaning and washing. Still, once he is fully potty trained, you will look back at this as just another learning experience of many.

CHAPTER 10. WHEN NOTHING WORKS (STEP-BY-STEP PLAN BASED ON A REAL STORY)

Sometimes nothing seems to work. The standard advice and all the methods seem to fail. It happens, and you're not the only one. There is no one plan that works 100 percent of the time, but your love as a parent is the key that overcomes everything. Remember that.

Let me tell you the story of my son, Bobby. His story is our story, and maybe someone will find it helpful because of similarities to their situation. And maybe our experience will help you to overcome one of the most difficult problems for parents and children — the problem of potty training.

Bobby was born premature at 35 weeks. He had to be resuscitated and the doctors saved his life. But because of all the antibiotics he had to take, he had problems having bowel movements. When he was two years old, he had a lot of problems with constipation, and he remembered it for a long time.

When we started potty training, these memories of that constipation were a problem. Bobby quickly learned to pee in the potty with no trouble, but... he was terribly afraid to sit down and poop on the potty.

We begged, pleaded, promised, offered rewards... but everything was useless: fear, stress, tears even enemas.

It is interesting that Bobby was already out of diapers, but he was afraid to poop on the potty. Because of that he would hold it for a few days. And even when he did try to poop, he failed.

Our struggle went on for a couple of months. Sometimes I

almost lost hope, and worried that our boy would have serious psychological trauma. But my husband, with his previous experience and support, was there for me and didn't let me down.

So, we read dozens of books and tried all the well-known tips and solutions. Finally, after two months our efforts paid off. Bobby pooped on the potty by himself!

And now he goes to the potty with such joy and pleasure. You should see his proud face! :)

So what did we do to help him? There wasn't just one simple solution, but instead a combination of seven important tips at the same time.

Here they are:

No Stress

Stop putting too much pressure on your child and don't worry. Try to let the problem go and decide not to panic.

The Right Equipment

We changed the potty chair, trying to pick out the most comfortable shape.

My opinion is that it is best to buy a potty chair without any toys or musical gadgets attached. You don't want your child to see the potty as a toy, because he might start using it for play and get distracted from the potty-training process.

As I mentioned before, you can try picking out and buying

the potty chair with your child. Let him decide which one he wants to use.

Next, we put the potty in a place that our son was happy with. You may even need to have the potty chair in the middle of your living room for some period of time! If your child is comfortable there, go with it! It's worth it, believe me!

Drinking Lots of Water

Please pay attention to one of the most important parts of healthy body development—hydration. And it's important for your child to not just drink juice and milk, he needs to drink water!!!

It's very important, especially in the morning when your child wakes up, to give him a glass of water and then afterward put him on the potty.

If your toddler is not used to drinking water, teach him little by little. Explain that this is very important and will help him be as strong, brave and quick as his favorite cartoon character. Or you can make it into a game.

It's good for your toddler to drink two to three cups of water a day, depending on his weight. You might want to buy him his own handy water bottle, which he could choose for himself.

Routine

It's easy to focus on trying to get your toddler to poop in the morning. After all, it's helpful to be in the routine and then the process of going poop at the preschool or daycare in the future will be easier.

But that isn't the most important thing. In our case, for example, at first Bobby only liked to poop in the evening.

At first he always waited until after dark. Later he got more comfortable with the potty and now uses it whenever he wants to.

Every time your child goes to use the potty, he should feel your support. Don't push him, and give him as much time as he needs, but at the same time don't let him sit for too long without any results.

High-fiber Foods

Pay attention, as we ended up doing, to nutrition. Our son really loved bread, muffins, chocolate, and cakes, all of which caused constipation and contributed to the potty problems.

That's why I made a list of foods that would be healthy for my child and stimulate the digestive system.

We replaced white flour with rye, wheat flour cookies with oatmeal, and began to give our son more vegetables and fruit. Let your toddler eat even two spoons full of vegetables, and they will be super useful and will do their work. Below I have an example of my menu.

Here are some of the foods that helped us: beets, carrots,

cauliflower and broccoli. Fresh apples, plums and watermelon. Lean fish and meat, baked potatoes, porridges, cereals, cereal flakes, dried fruit, olive oil as a dressing for salads, kefir/buttermilk, yogurt, low-fat cottage cheese.

The doctor suggested to us a baby probiotics course with vitamins. In our case, they seemed to be a good option and seemed to help.

Video Examples on Youtube

It was interesting for me to see how my husband helped our son with his potty problem. He showed him different videos.

A friend of mine advised me to show our son a video of children using the potty. She did that to help her little daughter learn to use the potty. But our son didn't like those videos at all.

So Daddy picked out some "special" videos just for him. Knowing how much he loves animals, such as tigers, cheetahs and other predators, my husband found videos on YouTube of these animals pooping and showed him.

Our son was really interested, and my husband explained that pooping isn't scary, that it's easy and doesn't hurt. Then the next time our son was sitting on the potty, he asked to see the video again.

Bobby looked at these animals pooping with interest. It was funny, but at the same time, we were really happy. And soon, Bobby started trying to go himself.

Rewards

And our last tactical and strategic step was to give rewards for our son's efforts. After each time that he successfully went potty, he immediately got a prize. We rewarded him with toys, sweets and cookies.

It's important to be moderate here. You can give just a small reward: one or two cookies or some small toy. Just enough to make the child happy and give him some extra motivation.

Hug and Poop Together

At first, it was hard for Bobby to push and poop. He was constantly worried about not being able to do it. To try to help get rid of his anxiety and fear we came up with one simple thing.

Remember the power of a parent's love?

It was intuitive and from the bottom of my heart. But it helped a lot.

What did we do? We just sat next to our son and hugged him when he was on the potty. Just some hugs helped him to feel our support, got rid of the fear, and helped him to push as hard as he needed to.

Later, he learned that he could go to the potty easily. He developed the necessary skills and reflexes and started to do things by himself. But in the early stages, those hugs were important for him.

Of course, the hugs don't have to come from the whole family. It can be just you, your husband or a person who your son trusts.

Ritual Farewell

Our family developed a funny ritual during potty training. It was important for our son to see the process as a game. It became interesting enough that he forgot his fears and emotional distress.

So every time our son finished "his business," we dumped the poop in the potty and said, "Bye-bye poop! Say hi to your friends for us!" and our little boy pressed the button and flushed it down the toilet. It was fun to watch him enjoying the whole process.

Repeat

You'll feel like you're in seventh heaven the first time everything works out, but it's important to consolidate the success. Keep repeating the steps for a few weeks.

Your efforts are sure to bear fruit! One day your toddler will surprise you and do everything by himself without your help.

Patience

Sometimes you may feel despair. Sometimes you'll feel angry with your child, and sometimes with yourself. But don't let despair win. Don't show your disappointment and don't be angry with your child.

Your child can feel the disappointment and anger, and he worries no less than you.

If you want to cry — cry, if you want to scream — scream. But do it in another room where you can't be seen or heard by your child. He needs support, understanding and love from you.

So, maybe this process will take you a few days or maybe a few weeks. Be patient and listen to your heart. Use all the tips that I've shared with you, and in time you will definitely succeed in this important challenge in your family life.

CHAPTER 11. WATER IS THE KEY

When your child grows up and starts eating solid food, his body needs more water. Also, the loss of fluid increases due to the increased activity of the child.

Water helps digestion. It prevents constipation and makes the pooping process much easier. That's exactly what we need for potty training!

A child needs three to five cups of water per day. Pure non-carbonated water. Juices, soda, milk, milkshakes, smoothies, tea, chocolate milk and other similar beverages don't count.

How Do You Teach a Child to Drink Water?

1. Children copy their parents' behavior. Drink water regularly, and your child will want to do the same.

2. Children like rituals. Start a "water" ritual—drink a glass

of water immediately when waking up and a few hours before bedtime. Always have your child drink water after pooping!

3. Make water always available. Always give your child water, wherever he goes. Keep water bottles around the house, especially in the bedroom and the living room.

Children are so busy all day long with playing and can forget about thirst. If your child doesn't like the taste of water, add some slices of lemon or lime for better flavor.

4. Try to tell your child as often as possible how important water is to his body. It is the source, not only of health, but also of beauty.

5. A glass of water before a walk, a glass of water after a walk.

6. Let your child drink water from a nice bottle with a favorite cartoon character or from a bright-colored bottle.

7. Make sure you give your child water whenever you offer him sweets, chocolate, cookies or desserts. Drinking water after having sweets will help to keep his teeth clean, and all of us want our kids' teeth to stay clean and intact.

CHAPTER 12. PECULIARITIES OF POTTY TRAINING FOR BOYS

Once you believe your little boy is ready, focus on the timing. Make sure your child's routine is well established. If he has just started daycare or has a little brother or sister, he may be less receptive to change or be too sensitive to take on this new challenge.

Let Him Watch and Learn

Little ones learn by imitation. Observing grown ups go to the toilet is, therefore, a natural first step. And that's where having a man at home is important. Following his father, uncle or family friend to the toilet to watch him pee can really help your boy become more familiar with the idea. He may notice that Dad and Mom do not use the toilet in the same way. This will give you the opportunity to explain how little boys go pee.

Buy the Right Equipment

Most experts advise you to buy a potty chair to which your toddler can make his own and will be more reassuring than using a big toilet (many children are afraid to fall into the toilet, and this anxiety can slow down their potty training progress).

If you prefer to buy a child's toilet seat that fits on your toilet seat, make sure it is comfortable and securely attached. If you choose this option, you will also need to purchase a step stool so that your child can easily climb up and down to and from the toilet when he needs to use it and can stabilize his legs when sitting. Another good way to facilitate learning is a good book or video that explains how to use the potty.

Help Your Child to Be Comfortable with the Potty

At this point, your boy should be familiar with the toilet. Start by making him understand that the potty chair or the potty seat belongs to him. You can personalize it by putting his name on it or by letting him decorate it with stickers.

A week later, you can suggest to him to take off his pants and underwear or diaper. If he refuses, don't force him. This will just create a power struggle that could throw off the whole process. If your child has a favorite doll or toy, use it to show him how to go on the potty. Kids love to see their favorite toy come alive and the explanation will have more impact than if it came from you. Some parents even make a little potty for the doll, so this way, everyone has his own potty!

Buy Him Big Boy Underwear

Draw your son's attention to the benefits of being clean by taking him on a special shopping trip: to buy his first real underwear! Tell him that he can choose the ones he wants (briefs or boxers with favorite cartoons or superheroes are always very popular).

Talk about this shopping day well in advance, so he will be intrigued at the idea of being big enough to go potty and wear "real" underwear just like his dad or his older brothers.

Establish a Learning Schedule for Potty Training

Being able to leave your child without a diaper will depend on your daily schedule. If you need someone else to watch your boy while you're busy, you will have to pass on your strategy to the daycare staff or babysitter. You will need to make a choice between diapers and underwear. If not wearing diapers is a practical option, many experts and parents prefer to put children directly into washable underwear that allow the child to feel right away when he is wet.

Of course, this will require you to clean up in the case of accidents. If you cannot decide on a method, talk to your pediatrician. For some time, it will be necessary to use disposable diapers or training pants at night and on long trips.

Teach Him to Pee Sitting down first, then standing up

As poop and pee often happen at the same time, it makes more sense to teach your son to sit down at first so he understands that everything goes into the potty. In this way, he will not try to play with his pee and learn to aim, while he is supposed to focus solely on mastering the basics of using the potty.

When your son seems comfortable on his potty or on his toilet seat, have him try the standing position on his little stool so it can be at the right height level. There is no reason to rush things. He can sit as long as he wants. If he seems reluctant to stand up, float a little toilet paper or other small object in the toilet bowl, and this can serve as a target. Expect to clean up around the toilet!

Leave Your Boy Half-dressed

By remaining only half dressed, your child can learn when he needs to go to the toilet. Place the potty in a place that is accessible from where he plays, and encourage him to sit on it from time to time. Watch for signals (if he puts his hand on his privates, squirms, or hops around), then suggest to him that he goes to the potty. You can do this over several consecutive days, in the evening, when the family is all together, or just weekends, as you see fit. The longer your child spends without being fully clothed, the faster he will learn.

CHAPTER 13. CELEBRATION AND REWARDS

It's important to understand the difference between a reward and a bribe. The line can get a bit blurry here, but the essential difference is this: A reward follows the behavior you're trying to reinforce, and a bribe precedes it. Also, a reward should be given as soon as possible after the behavior that is being rewarded, in order to make a firm association between the behavior and the positive reinforcement.

You know that excitement you feel when you receive the signal from your son or daughter that they are ready to potty train? The signal you've been patiently waiting for forever? Well, maybe not forever, but for a long time. Some children, especially as they near the age of three, can be motivated to use the potty if offered a reward afterward. Stickers, small prizes, a trip to the library or the park, or playing a favorite game together may work well if your child is ready to potty train anyway. The reward motivates a child to keep practicing skills that might otherwise be less interesting to him.

Every child will be easier to motivate with rewards and will more cheerfully complete the task at hand for a little Potty-Training Celebration when he's done. If rewards or a fun motivation works for your child, here are some Potty-Training Celebration Ideas. Potty training is a big deal for you and your child, and using a reward system is a great way to promote potty-training success.

1. Sticker Chart

There's something very exciting to a young child about choosing a sticker and placing it in a particular spot. And seeing those stickers accumulate over time is a great visual reminder of what a great job they're doing!

2. Potty Treats Jar

Grab a jar and fill it with a favorite small candy. Whether it's suckers, jellybeans, M&Ms or Skittles, you may find that a little candy can go a long way toward encouraging your child to stay dry during the day.

3. Potty Prizes

If candy isn't your thing, head to the dollar store and create a potty prize box. Every time your child pees or poops on the potty, he gets to grab a new toy to play with.

Or, offer larger gifts as an incentive for earning stickers on your child's sticker chart. Maybe they get to pick out a toy at the store over the weekend if they use the potty all week.

If your child loves to have friends over, you could allow him to host a playdate on Saturday if he stays dry all day on Friday. Or maybe let him pick what the family eats for dinner if he has only one accident during the day. You know your child better than anyone, and you know what will motivate him to use the potty.

Advice from Parents: Start Small!

As you're deciding what rewards to offer for potty training, parents who have been there before you will advise you to start small. If your child is thrilled with the "reward" of flushing the toilet every time he uses it, then there's no need to waste your money on toys or candy.

If your son is so excited that he gets one piece of candy when he pees, there's no need to offer him ten pieces. Start small and slowly increase your rewards if necessary to motivate your kids. This will save you from making a trip to the toy store every single time your child uses the potty!

CHAPTER 14. EAT, PLAY, POOP, REPEAT

Potty training a child successfully and quickly does not happen accidentally. Rather, parents who want to potty train a child in a matter of days must arm themselves with a time-tested system and a well-thought-out plan of action that builds their self-confidence and allows them to tap into their strengths and avoid the most common and costly pitfalls.

It is important to review all the tips of potty training for boys but, if you have a strong-willed child and you're convinced that potty training him is likely to become a contest of wills, or you're already frustrated after one or more unsuccessful attempts at potty training your child, know that you're not alone.

As a parent, you need to know that there is no fixed time for potty training. You need to observe the general tendencies of your child to look for readiness to use the potty. The process may be very tiring but you need to have patience. Tell and show your son about how using the potty works. You might want to use a doll to demonstrate different potty habits.

Your child will need you to be confident, calm and focused on him for the scheduled potty-training session. Decide when you want to do the initial training and clear your calendar for a few days during that time. Make sure there are no overly stressful events going on in your child's life during potty training time. If your family life is currently difficult or chaotic, put off training your little potty trainee until things calm down, if possible.

It is important to repeat the potty-training process until your child is toilet trained.

✓ Prepare your child. Talk to him about what you'll be teaching him.

✓ Let your child watch you use the bathroom. Modeling is important!

✓ Give your child plenty of fluids throughout the potty-training day.

✓ Take him to the potty chair regularly, every one to two hours. Eventually, something will happen in the potty chair!

✓ Make a big deal out of his successes. Be matter-of-fact about everything else.

✓ Repeat this process until your child is toilet trained.

✓ Realize the initial training may take only a few days, but making the process a habit will take months.

If your child is having a lot of accidents, it is often effective to let him wear underwear, but then put a pull-up on top of the underwear. If he has an accident, the underwear will still get wet, which he will feel.

Pull-ups often absorb so much that the child doesn't have the feeling of being wet, which is an important part of potty training. The reason you put a pull-up over the underwear is to protect his clothes, and his classroom if he is in school, from getting wet. Teachers will appreciate that!

Remind the teachers to encourage your child to go to the potty periodically. Kids get so involved in play that they often forget to go the bathroom until it's too late. Teachers should encourage the child to at least try to go, and should praise them for the attempt.

In the classroom, it is good if children are allowed to go to the bathroom whenever they need to. While potty training, some kids go repeatedly, which is fine. Over time, the child will better understand as he keeps repeating this process when he really needs to go and the frequency will diminish.

CHAPTER 15. DEALING WITH ACCIDENTS

Accidents need to be dealt with quietly and calmly. You also need to learn to read your boy's signals so you know when he needs to go to the bathroom. It will take both of you working together for the potty training to be successful.

Let's say everything is moving along nicely. Your little one seems to have mastered potty training and you think you've said goodbye to diapers for good. But then he suddenly starts having accidents again, and you wonder what went wrong. Often, accidents happen because a child is having too much fun playing or doing an activity and just doesn't want to stop to run to the bathroom.

Rest assured that plenty of kids experience potty training regression—it is completely normal. But you may need to ask yourself whether your child was ever really potty trained in the first place. It is very common for occasional setbacks in the early days, months, or even years of potty training. But a child who has several accidents every day and doesn't seem to care about them should not really be considered "potty trained." So, consider whether your child was ready to potty train. If he was, start looking for ways to get back on track. If not, talk to your pediatrician about when he or she thinks your child might be ready.

If your child has an accident, don't show disappointment; doing so can make your little one more anxious and that, in turn, can lead to more potty problems. Despite the frustration of having to head back into having accidents, and maybe having to use diapers because of toilet-training regression, do everything you can to stay positive. When you check to see if your child is dry, clap and cheer if he is. If he's not, just remain nonjudgmental and say, "Oops. You had an accident. Let's go sit on the potty." Remember to remain upbeat and never yell at or scold your child. You want your children to feel empowered and not worry that they're going to be punished if they make a mistake.

You're not going to stop the setbacks if you don't address the exact problem. Try to identify the reasons for the regression, since addressing them will help the child return to where he was. For instance, many children start having accidents during times of transition that might cause stress, such as starting a new school or welcoming a new sibling. If that is the case, chances are when your lives settle down, your child will master potty training once again. But even if your child makes it through the day without accidents, he still may have mishaps at night. Many kids are not dry at night for years after they are dry during the day. Medical issues can also cause potty training accidents, and constipation is a common one. If a child has difficulty having a bowel movement, he might steer clear of the potty altogether to avoid having to push and strain. Make sure your child is getting enough fiber and plenty of water, but if he's scared of pooping on the potty, play games or read books with him while he sits on the toilet to make it more fun. Encourage your child to at least try to use the potty when he first wakes up, before meals, before bedtime, and immediately before you leave the house to go anywhere.

BONUS CHAPTER 16. 41 TIPS FOR MODERN PARENTS FOR SUCCESSFUL POTTY TRAINING

✓ In the beginning, keep a constant eye on your child or he will go anywhere.

✓ Potty training a child who is ready is quite simple with the right techniques and attitude. The number one most important tip is to make it fun for the child and to not make a big deal of accidents. When your child has successfully used the potty, whether it is the first time or the 20th time, make a huge deal about it. Give him a reward, but it doesn't necessarily need to be a tangible reward—it can be lots of clapping, jumping up and down, or lots of praising.

Kids will normally do whatever it takes to make their mom happy but they will also do whatever it takes to get a big reaction out of their parents. If they have an accident, and the parent makes a big fuss over it, it will happen again and again. However, if the accident is ignored, no attention is given to the accident nor mention is made of it at all, then it becomes a passing memory and is unlikely to happen more often than successful potty trips.

✓ Another good tip is to stop using diapers and don't even start using other types of disposable training pants. Instead, go straight to cloth training pants, preferably with a favorite cartoon character that way they won't want to poop or pee on their favorite character.

✓ Establish a reward system that lets your child earn a treat or badge of some sort when he successfully "accomplishes his mission." Chocolate always seems to be an appreciated reward, but some parents may prefer giving stickers and small toys, or using a chart.

✓ Remember that your son's first milestone to be rewarded will be that he has learned to equate the dirty diaper with the potty. Specifically, he might communicate to you that he needs to potty after he already used his diaper. This is an important first step!

✓ Turn potty training into a simple game. Indulge his emerging interest in music, football or basketball by using a musical or sports-themed potty chair. There are some great products available, which are designed to make potty training fun, like the Flush and Cheer Potty Chair.

✓ Continue the games to keep his interest as he matures. When he reaches the point of successfully going to pee, let your son experience the innate masculine pleasure of aiming at things floating in the potty. One or two rings of cereal from a box of Cheerios always make a handy target, and they won't clog up your plumbing.

✓ Consider the act of flushing the potty to be a reward in itself. This not only motivates your child to actually go potty on the toilet, but also reinforces the importance of only flushing when necessary. It is never too early to begin taking steps to prevent the misfortune of a plumber's expense if your son flushes something inappropriate down the toilet.

✓ As he progresses through the training phase, your little boy should no longer be sleeping in a crib, but should be in a toddler bed so he can climb out and use the potty when he needs to during naps and overnight.

✓ Stop using disposable diapers or disposable training pants. These products are designed to make your child comfortable after he soils himself. This is exactly what you do not want during potty training. Instead, use cloth diapers or traditional plastic training pants to cover his "big boy underwear." The more uncomfortable he is when he forgets to use the potty, the faster he will work through the toilet-training stage.

✓ Have your son spend time with an older child or another toddler who is already toilet trained who can encourage him to "be a big boy" by using the potty. Peer learning and mentoring concepts are very effective for potty training boys.

✓ In the summertime, let your son "pee on a tree" like his dad or older brother does when they are outdoors. Few things can make a little boy feel more "manly" than this, and he will enjoy the satisfaction of knowing that he can do this instead of using his diaper or pull-up.

✓ To get your child to sit still long enough to "go number two," sit beside him and read him a book about potty training. Many books have been published for precisely this purpose and children love them.

✓ Take your child to the store and let them pick out their own potty chair.

✓ Encourage him to decorate it with stickers and drawings to make it feel more like his own.

✓ Start by just letting him sit on it whenever he wants, for whatever reason. He may want to read a book while sitting on his potty, he may also want to use the potty with his diaper on. Just sitting on it will help him be more comfortable.

✓ Make potty time a routine. Set specific times your child sits on the potty for a few minutes; whether or not they actually use it doesn't matter.

✓ At other than the designated times, if they show signs of needing to go, rush them to the potty chair and reward them if they do successfully use the chair.

✓ Try NOT to get mad when they have an accident. This

process takes time and practice and children should be rewarded for successes, not punished for failures.

✓ When your child does a "poo-poo" in their diaper, help them take it to the potty chair. That will tell them where the "poo-poo" goes.

✓ It's going to take time. On average, potty training a boy can take a few months, so don't rush things and be patient.

✓ Don't yell. Face reality and understand that your son is going to have accidents. Don't yell or belittle him, as it will send things backwards.

✓ Take aim. Sometimes getting a boy to aim into the toilet properly can be a challenge in itself.

✓ Standing or sitting? Some parents have their sons start sitting down to pee, so there is less confusion for them with the overall process.

✓ Let him watch Dad. Kids learn by watching, so don't hesitate to let your toddler watch Dad or an older brother use the toilet.

✓ Drop your shorts. Be sure to put clothing on boys that are easy to remove while they are toilet training.

✓ Be patient. One way of making this whole process easier is to take a relaxed attitude toward it—accept that training might take a long time.

✓ Reminders. Little kids have to pee very often, so be sure to ask them at least every 30 minutes if they have to go.

✓ Be open-minded and flexible. It is easy to get confused with the mass of (often contradictory) potty training advice out there. Trying to decide which is the best method is not always easy.

✓ Timing. There is a saying among experts that if you start a child potty training at the age of two, they will achieve control by the age of three.

✓ Let your toddler take the lead. Don't force toilet training upon your child.

✓ Some practical tips. If you live in a two-story house, buy two identical potties to avoid cries of "I want the other potty" and the subsequent toilet training accidents as your little one races to the favored potty chair.

✓ Books and video. Take the time to include a few potty training story books into reading time with your toddler well before you intend to start the training.

✓ Sticker chart and rewards. Get creative when you decide on the reward system you are going to use to motivate your toddler toward toileting independence.

✓ Toilet targets. Put Cheerios or a ping-pong ball into the toilet bowl for little boys to aim at.

✓ Take them shopping for underwear. Being able to choose his own "real" underwear is very exciting for most children.

✓ Toy or teddy bear. Use an existing toy or teddy bear and put a small diaper on it so that your child has a friend to go through the training with.

✓ Decorate the potty. Let your son decorate his own potty using stickers. He will be anxious to use it because he will be so proud of it.

✓ Support team. Ensure that your friends and family know potty training is underway.

✓ Make the bathroom welcoming. Bathrooms tend to be very functional (out of necessity). Put a couple of small toys and books in there to keep your son occupied during the times that he is sitting on the potty.

✓ Fun food. Constipation is a common problem for potty training children. Ensure their diet has been modified so that constipation-promoting foods (including processed foods) are kept to a minimum. You may need to introduce new foods such as fresh fruits and vegetables. Make these more appealing by cutting them into fun shapes either with a knife or cookie cutters.

REFERENCES

6 Things Every Parent Should Know About Toilet Training. (2018, March 30). Retrieved from https://www. nationwidechildrens.org/family-resources-education/ 700childrens/2018/03/6-things-every-parent-should-know-about-toilet-training

Ceder, J. (2020, April 6). How To Potty Train Your Child in 3 Just Days. Retrieved from https://www.verywellfamily. com/three-day-potty-training-tips-4071189

Kim, L. (2020, February 6). How to De-Stress at Work Instantly: 15 Proven Ways to Calm Your Mind. Retrieved from https://www.inc.com/larry-kim/how-to-de-stress-at-work-instantly-15-proven-ways-to-calm-your-mind.html

Making a Healthier Homemade Pizza. (2015, May 1).

Retrieved from https://www.disabled-world.com/fitness/nutrition/pizza.php

Nazish, N. (2019, May 31). How To De-Stress In 5 Minutes Or Less, According To A Navy SEAL. Retrieved from https://www.forbes.com/sites/nomanazish/2019/05/30/how-to-de-stress-in-5-minutes-or-less-according-to-a-navy-seal/#38255f953046-

NHS. (n.d.). How much salt do babies and children need? Retrieved from https://www.nhs.uk/common-health-questions/childrens-health/how-much-salt-do-babies-and-children-need/

Shaw, G. (2012, January 21). A Nutritionist Speaks: How to Promote Your Child's Digestive Health. Retrieved from https://www.webmd.com/children/features/digestive-health#1

Westbrooks, E. (2018, April 6). How To Potty Train In 2 Days, Because You're Feeling Brave. Retrieved from https://www.romper.com/p/how-to-potty-train-in-2-days-because-youre-feeling-brave-8711571

CPSIA information can be obtained
at www.ICGtesting.com
Printed in the USA
LVHW030607100221
678886LV00006B/581